THE SACRED TRIANGLE

AYODYA-NAIMISARANYAM-VARANASI

PRABHAKAR VEERARAGHAVAN

The Sacred Triangle Naimisaranyam – Ayodya - Varanasi

Journeying Through India's Holiest Cities

By : Prabhakar Veeraraghavan

1. Exploring the Spiritual Heartland of India
2. Journeys Through India's Holiest Cities
3. Myths, Legends, and Divine Tales
4. Pilgrimage Pathways and Sacred Sites
5. A Deep Dive into India's Sacred Geography
6. Cultural and Religious Tapestry of Ancient India
7. Mythical Histories and Timeless Traditions
8. Unveiling the Divine Mysteries
9. A Sacred Journey through History and Myth
10. The Eternal Cities of Faith and Tradition

About the author

PRABHAKAR VEERARAGHAVAN is a Blogger and an accomplished KDP Author and Seller after spending more than 2 decades in the corporate world. Passionate in Travelling and writing books with an innate ability to transport readers to captivating words and evoke profound emotions, Prabhakar has put in all his experience into words that can benefit many readers.

ALL RIGHTS RESERVED

I. Introduction

In the heartland of India, where the river Ganges flows with timeless grace, lies a tapestry of ancient cities, each woven with threads of myth, legend, and spirituality. Among these, Ayodhya, Naimisaranyam, and Varanasi stand as sanctuaries of profound significance, bearing witness to epochs of history, culture, and faith.

Ayodhya

Ayodhya, the legendary birthplace of Lord Rama, resonates with the echoes of the Ramayana, one of the greatest epics ever told. Nestled on the banks of the sacred Sarayu River, this ancient city carries a serene aura, drawing pilgrims and seekers from far and wide. From the grandeur of the Ram Janmabhoomi Temple to the tranquil environs of Hanuman Garhi, every corner of Ayodhya breathes the essence of devotion and reverence.

NAIMISARANYAM

In the mystical forests of Naimisaranyam, time seems to stand still, as if caught in the embrace of divine contemplation. This sacred grove, where the Vedas are said to have been narrated by the sage Veda Vyasa, exudes an aura of profound spirituality. Amidst the whispering leaves and ancient temples, pilgrims embark on a journey of introspection and enlightenment, seeking solace in the sanctity of this hallowed ground.

VARANASI

Varanasi, the eternal city of light, stands as a beacon of spiritual awakening amidst the ebb and flow of existence. Revered as the holiest of the seven sacred cities in Hinduism, Varanasi is a kaleidoscope of colors, sounds, and sensations. From the ghats that line the sacred Ganges River to the labyrinthine lanes of the old city, every corner of Varanasi pulsates with the rhythm of devotion and transcendence. Here, life and death intertwine in a timeless dance, inviting pilgrims to embrace the eternal cycle of creation and dissolution.

Introduction

In the sacred heartland of India, where the timeless Ganges meanders through landscapes steeped in history and spirituality, lie three ancient cities — Naimisaranyam, Ayodhya, and Varanasi. Each city holds its own unique allure, beckoning pilgrims and travelers to embark on a journey of discovery and devotion.

Naimisaranyam:

Our pilgrimage begins amidst the tranquil forests of Naimisaranyam, where the echoes of ancient hymns and timeless wisdom reverberate through the trees. This sacred grove, believed to be the abode where the sage Veda Vyasa recited the Vedas, serves as a sanctuary for seekers and pilgrims. From the towering temple spires to the whispering leaves of the sacred banyan tree, every corner of Naimisaranyam exudes an aura of divine grace and introspection.

Ayodhya:

From Naimisaranyam, our journey takes us to the legendary city of Ayodhya, cradle of the revered deity Lord Rama. Nestled along the banks of the holy Sarayu River, Ayodhya unfolds like a tapestry of myth and legend, its streets steeped in the stories of ancient epics. Here, amidst the grandeur of the Ram

Janmabhoomi Temple and the tranquility of Hanuman Garhi, pilgrims find solace in the embrace of devotion and reverence.

Varanasi:

Our pilgrimage culminates in the timeless city of Varanasi, where life and death converge in a symphony of spirituality and existence. Revered as the holiest of the seven sacred cities in Hinduism, Varanasi captivates the soul with its labyrinthine lanes and ancient ghats. From the ethereal glow of dawn on the Ganges to the mesmerizing chants of evening aarti, every moment in Varanasi is a testament to the eternal dance of creation and dissolution.

Conclusion:

As we journey from the sacred groves of Naimisaranyam to the hallowed precincts of Ayodhya and finally to the eternal city of Varanasi, let us tread lightly, with hearts open to the whispers of the divine. For in these ancient cities, where the past merges seamlessly with the present, we may find not only a glimpse of eternity but also the essence of our own souls.

DELHI – LUCKNOW – NAIMISARANYAM – AYODYA – VARANASI – DELHI
NAIMISARANYAM

By Train :

Travelling from Delhi to Naimisaranyam by Road is the convenient way of travelling, as lot of trains runs between Delhi to Lucknow and I have chosen the vehicle **New Delhi – LKO AC Express which runs at 23.05 Hrs at New Delhi and reaches Lucknow at 07.25 AM**. It runs on all days of the week i.e from Monday to Sunday from Delhi which is a very convenient train not affecting the office goers with offers at an economical rate of Rs. 775 for per person in 3rd AC Three tier sleeper which is very convenient to travel.

You can book these tickets through IRCTC.com wherein you will be able to get the confirmed accommodation ticket. You can get all the famous trains like Vande Bharat Express starting at 06.10 a.m. at New Delhi and reaching Lucknow at 12.25 pm. But this train will not suit you because of the distance. Also, other trains like IRCTC Tejas express, at 15.50 pm., DBRG Rajdhani which starts at 11.25 pm and reaches at 18.40 pm. and so on.

Overall, the total distance from Lucknow to Naimisaranyam by road is approximately 315 kilometres, and the journey can take around 8 to 11 hours in total, depending on factors such as traffic and road conditions. It's advisable to check the route and road conditions before starting your journey, and it's always a good idea to carry necessary provisions for a comfortable trip.

By Bus :

Traveling from Delhi to Lucknow by bus is a popular and convenient option. Here's a general guide on how to do it:

1. Selecting a Bus Service:

There are several private and state-run bus services operating between Delhi and Lucknow. You can choose from various options based on your budget, comfort preferences, and departure timings. Some popular bus operators on this route include UPSRTC, RSRTC, and private operators like Volvo, AC, and sleeper buses.

2. Booking Tickets:

Once you've chosen the bus service, you can book your tickets. You can book tickets online through the respective bus operator's website or through third-party ticketing platforms. Alternatively, you can visit the bus terminal or travel agencies in Delhi to purchase tickets in person.

3. Departure Points in Delhi:

Buses from Delhi to Lucknow usually depart from major bus terminals such as the Interstate Bus Terminal (ISBT) in Kashmiri Gate, Anand Vihar Terminal, or Sarai Kale Khan Terminal. Make sure to arrive at the departure point well in advance to avoid any last-minute rush.

4. Travel Duration:

The travel duration from Delhi to Lucknow by bus varies depending on factors such as traffic, road conditions, and the type of bus. Generally, the journey takes around 8 to 10 hours to cover the distance of approximately 500 to 550 kilometers.

5. Arrival Points in Lucknow:

Buses from Delhi typically arrive at major bus terminals in Lucknow, such as Alambagh Bus Station, Charbagh Bus Station, or the newly built Integrated Bus Terminal (ISBT) at Sarojini Nagar. From these terminals, you can easily access other parts of

Lucknow through local transport options like auto-rickshaws or taxis.

6. Comfort and Amenities:

Depending on the type of bus you choose, amenities may vary. Some buses offer features like air conditioning, reclining seats, onboard entertainment, and restroom facilities. Make sure to check the amenities provided by the bus operator before booking your ticket.

7. Safety and Security:

While traveling, ensure your belongings are secure, and follow safety guidelines provided by the bus operator. Keep your valuables with you and be vigilant during rest stops or layovers.

By following these steps, you can easily travel from Delhi to Lucknow by bus and enjoy a comfortable journey to your destination.

By Flight :

Traveling from Delhi to Lucknow by air is a convenient option due to the availability of regular flights between the two cities. Here's a general guide on how to do it:

1. Selecting a Flight:

Numerous airlines operate flights between Delhi and Lucknow, offering a range of options in terms of timings, prices, and services. You can choose from full-service carriers, low-cost airlines, and regional airlines based on your preferences and budget.

2. Booking Tickets:

Once you've selected your preferred flight, you can book your tickets online through the airline's website or mobile app. Alternatively, you can use third-party travel booking platforms to compare prices and make reservations. It's advisable to book your tickets in advance to secure better deals and ensure seat availability, especially during peak travel seasons.

3. Departure from Delhi:

Flights from Delhi to Lucknow usually depart from the Indira Gandhi International Airport (DEL), which is one of the busiest airports in India. Ensure to arrive at the airport well before your scheduled departure time to complete check-in procedures, security screening, and other formalities.

4. Flight Duration:

The flight duration from Delhi to Lucknow is relatively short, typically ranging from 1 to 1.5 hours, depending on factors such as the airline, aircraft type, and weather conditions. Flights cover a distance of approximately 400 to 450 kilometers.

5. Arrival in Lucknow:

Upon arrival at Lucknow, flights land at the Chaudhary Charan Singh International Airport (LKO). The airport is located around 13 kilometers from the city center. From the airport, you can easily access various modes of transportation such as taxis, app-based cab services, and airport shuttles to reach your final destination in Lucknow.

By following these steps, you can easily travel from Delhi to Lucknow by air and enjoy a comfortable and efficient journey to your destination.

After arrival in Lucknow:

Check-in Hotel Alpha, Opposite Pandariba Post Office, Pandariba Road, Charbagh, Lucknow. Contact person : Hardeep – Mobile 9161931767. You may check in to any of the booked hotels in Lucknow preferably near the railway station so that you can reach the railway station early the next day to

Ayodha. So ideally keep your luggage, and take bath and after having a small rest proceed to Naimisanyam temple.

It is to be noted that from Naimisaranyam it takes about half an hour to reach Kesar Bagh which is ideal place for travelling to many nearest station like Nainisaranyam etc.

It is to be noted that the travel to Naimisaranyam takes 3 Hours only and if started in the morning it will be good and hence I have chosen the train that reaches Nainisaranyam only in the morning.

Please note that the last bus from Naimisaranyam to Lucknow is at 5.00 p.m and you need to be there at the Naimisaranyam Bus stand at that time.

After reaching Naimisaranyam, Just speak to any e-auto wala for a detailed and thorough trip and return the e-auto sala by 5.pm. at any cost so that you do not miss the bus in having the follow-up of same route to Lucknow bus stand.

Day-1 Trip To Naimisaranyam

Arrive at Naimisharanya and first visit Chakra Teerth.

Chakrateerth, located in Naimisharanya in the Sitapur district of Uttar Pradesh, is a significant Hindu pilgrimage site steeped in mythology and history. According to legend, it is the place where Lord Brahma's chakra (disc) fell, creating a sacred pond known as Chakrateerth. This event marked the spot as a focal point for spiritual activities and cosmic significance.

The origin of Chakrateerth is linked to a story where sages, troubled by demons, sought a peaceful place for penance. They approached Lord Brahma, who sent his chakra to guide them. The chakra eventually fell at Naimisharanya, indicating it as the sacred site free from the influence of Kaliyuga (the age of darkness and corruption). Here, the sages performed extensive penance and spiritual practice.

Naimisharanya is also significant for its association with various Hindu scriptures. It is believed that the great sage Vyasadeva composed the Vedas, Puranas, and other sacred texts at this location. Additionally, the first recital of the Satyanarayan Katha is said to have taken place here.

The site is surrounded by other notable religious locations, making it a vital pilgrimage destination. It is believed that a holy dip in the waters of Chakrateerth can purify one's mind, body, and soul.

Naimisharanya's historical and spiritual importance is further underscored by its mention in various ancient texts and its role as a sanctuary for sages and seekers throughout history. Naimisaranya, also known as Naimisharanya or Nimsar, is a sacred pilgrimage site in Uttar Pradesh, India, rich in history and mythology.

According to legend, it was on this holy land that Maharishi Vyas created Vedas and Puranas. It is believed that the interaction between Maharishi Shaunak and Soot happened near this place. Besides, in a congregation of 84,000 seers here, Soot narrated various Puranas and stories of the Mahabharat for 12 years. It is mentioned in the Matsya Mahapurana: Sutmekagramseenam

Naimisharanyamvasinah. Puran Mandir - Ma Anandmayi Ashram : Near Vyasgaddi are ancient Vatvriksha, Vyas Vatika, Odiya Baba temple, Jagadbandhu Ashram, and ashrams of Manu, Shatrupa and sage Kashyapa.

Major Attractions Around Naimisharanya

Naimisharanya is a hub of religious and historical significance, with numerous sacred sites attracting devotees and pilgrims. Here are some of the must-visit holy places in Naimisharanya:

1. Chakra Teerth:

Believed to have been created by the disc (chakra) emanating from Lord Brahma's heart, Chakra Teerth is a sacred pond where bathing is said to absolve all sins. It is the central attraction of Naimisharanya and holds great spiritual importance.

2. Vyas Gaddi

This is the place where Ved Vyasa compiled the Puranas and split the Vedas into four parts. It is a revered spot for scholars and devotees alike, who come to pay homage to the sage and his monumental contributions to Hindu scriptures.

3. Sri Lalita Devi Temple

This temple is one of the Shaktipeeths in India, marking the spot where the heart of Sati, wife of Lord Shiva, is believed to have fallen. It is a significant pilgrimage site, especially for devotees of the Goddess.

4. Balaji Temple

Dedicated to Lord Venkateshwara (Balaji), this temple is particularly popular among devotees from Andhra Pradesh. The temple provides accommodation for pilgrims, making it a convenient place to stay while visiting Naimisharanya.

5. Dadheechi Kund

According to legend, this kund (pond) is where Sage Dadheechi gave up his bones to create the weapon Vajra, which was used to kill the demon Vritrasura. Bathing in this kund is believed to be equivalent to bathing in all holy rivers and spots in India◇?◇9†source◇?◇.

6. Suth Gaddi

This site commemorates the sage Suth, a disciple of Ved Vyasa, who is said to have discoursed to 88,000 sages here. It is a place of profound spiritual learning and reflection.

7. Hanuman Gaddi and Pandav Killa:

Hanuman Gaddi is believed to be the spot where Hanuman freed Ram and Lakshman after killing the demon Ahiravan. The Pandavas are also said to have performed penance at Pandav Killa, making it a site of dual significance. It offers panoramic views of the surrounding area and is a popular pilgrimage site for devotees of Lord Hanuman.

8. Dasaashwamedha Ghat

This is the site where Lord Rama performed his tenth Ashwamedha Yagna. The ghat features an ancient temple with idols of Lord Rama, Lakshman, and Sita, marking it as an important pilgrimage spot.

9. Swayambhu Manu and Satrupa

This is the location where Swayambhu Manu and his wife Satrupa performed penance for 23,000 years to have Lord Narayana born as their son. It is a place of deep historical and spiritual significance.

10. Pancha Pandava Temple:

This temple is dedicated to the five Pandava brothers from the Mahabharata - Yudhishthira, Bhima, Arjuna, Nakula, and Sahadeva. It is believed to be the spot where the Pandavas performed penance during their exile.

Additional Information

Temple Timings

Open from 5 am to 9 pm, with a closure period between 12 pm and 4 pm.

Best Time to Visit

The best time to visit Naimisharanya is during the winter months from September to February, when the weather is cooler and more pleasant compared to the hot and humid summer months.

These attractions collectively make Naimisharanya a vital pilgrimage destination, deeply rooted in mythology and history, drawing visitors seeking spiritual enrichment and connection with ancient traditions.

IT SEEMS LIKE YOU'RE referring to Chakra Teerth in Naimisaranya (also known as Naimisharanya or Naimisha), an ancient pilgrimage site in Uttar Pradesh, India.

Chakra Teerth is a sacred site within Naimisaranya, believed to be the spot where Lord Vishnu's Sudarshana Chakra (divine discus) fell. It holds significant religious importance for Hindus. The entire Naimisaranya region is steeped in mythology and is associated with various ancient texts and legends.

Visiting Chakra Teerth in Naimisaranya can be a spiritually enriching experience for devotees and tourists alike. The site is often visited by pilgrims seeking blessings and divine grace. Chakra Teerth is nothing like visiting a place of sacred feeling and it helps you to pass the circle through knew depth water allowing the water to pass through the entire body.

If you're planning to visit Chakra Teerth and other sacred sites in Naimisaranya, it's advisable to research local travel information, including transportation options, accommodation facilities, and any specific guidelines or rituals associated with the pilgrimage. Additionally, considering its historical and religious significance, being respectful of the site's customs and traditions is essential during your visit.

Then proceed to Baba Bhutteswarnath Temple, Soot Gaddi Temple, and Lalitha Devi Temple. (5 Minutes Walk). Lalitha Devi Temple is a Hindu temple dedicated to Goddess Lalita Tripura Sundari, a form of the Divine Mother. The temple is located in Naimisaranya, Uttar Pradesh, India.

Halt here for a lunch at Shri Vaishno Bhojnalaya and after lunch proceed to auto for visiting other places..

NOW VISIT OTHER PLACES of interest viz. Vyaas Ghaddi, Akshay Vatt, Hanuman Garhi, Pandav Kila, Khatu Shyam Temple.

Gomti Ghaat, Tri Shakti Dham (South Indian Vishno Temple), Tirupathi Balaji Temple, Kali Shakti Peet.

Other Places : if time permits : Dadichi Kund (12 Kms). Then the E-Rickshaw flows to the same place as before and drops the entire troupe before 5,00 p.m. from where the bus stopped at Nainisaranyam in the morning. Then the bus returns to Kaiser Bagh in Lucknow.

Return to Kaiser Bagh and take a bus to Lucknow back to the Hotel. Have Dinner and Halt tonight.

Day 2 Trip - Ayodya

<u>**AYODYA TRIP**</u>

It seems like you've provided a comprehensive guide on how to reach Ayodhya by air, road, and train. Here's a summary:

By Air:

Ayodhya has its own airport inaugurated by Prime Minister Narendra Modi in December 2023.

The airport serves both Ayodhya and Faizabad and offers daily direct flights from various cities like Delhi, Ahmedabad, Bengaluru, and Kolkata.

If direct flights aren't available, you can fly into Lucknow's Chaudhary Charan Singh International Airport, which is about 130 km away from Ayodhya.

By Road:

Ayodhya is easily accessible by road with well-developed routes.

Private and public bus services operate from major cities like Delhi, Lucknow, Allahabad, and Gorakhpur.

Various options are available including low-budget non-AC buses to luxury Volvo buses.

Hiring a taxi or driving yourself are also convenient options for reaching Ayodhya by road.

By Train:

- Ayodhya is well-connected by rail with a busy railway station.
- Trains run from major Indian cities and towns to Ayodhya.
- Regular passenger trains operate between Ayodhya and nearby stations like Gorakhpur and Allahabad.
- Train travel to Ayodhya is economical and comfortable, with various ticket options available.

Overall, Ayodhya offers multiple transportation options making it easily accessible to visitors throughout the year. Whether you prefer traveling by air, road, or train, reaching Ayodhya is convenient and straightforward, allowing you to explore its rich history, temples, and monuments at your leisure.

It's great to know that Ayodhya offers excellent internal connectivity options for tourists. Here's a summary of the various modes of transportation available within the city:

Auto Rickshaws:

◈ Auto rickshaws are popular and easily available in Ayodhya.

◈ They provide a convenient and exciting way to explore the city.

Battery Operated Rickshaws:

◈ Battery-operated rickshaws have largely replaced traditional cycle rickshaws in Ayodhya.

◈ They are plentiful and easy to hire, offering a comfortable and eco-friendly way to travel.

E-Buses:

◈ Ayodhya is set to introduce 150 e-buses for local transportation.

◈ These buses will be especially useful for tourists visiting the Ram Mandir and other attractions in the city.

Taxis:

◈ Taxis are available for hire in Ayodhya.
◈ You can book taxis online or through local taxi hire agencies.
◈ They can also be included in Ayodhya holiday packages for convenience.

Golf Carts:

◈ Golf carts are available for transportation within the Ram Mandir premises.

◈ Priority is given to senior citizens and disabled individuals.

From Railway Station take an e-rickshaw and proceed to Ravat Mandhir Dharamshala, Ram Ghat Railway Bridge, Ram Katha Park, Ayodhya, Uttar Pradesh – 224123, 08069266018 / 8127425738.

Opposite to current hotel is a South Indian Café where you can get all types of South Indian Food like rice, idli Dosa,

Sambar etc. and you can fill your stomach by taking some South Indian Dishes over here.

Hanumangarhi, Ayodhya Overview

Weather : 27 - 37°C

Tags : Temple

Timings : 5:00 AM - 11:00 PM

Time Required : 2-3 hrs

Located in Sai Nagar, Hanuman Garhi is a 10th-century temple dedicated to the Hindu God, Hanuman. It is one of the most important temples in Ayodhya as it is customary to visit Hanuman Garhi before visiting the Ram Temple in Ayodhya. It is believed that Lord Hanuman lived at the temple site guarding Ayodhya.

The hilltop temple hones a 76-staircase pathway to the entrance. Housed within the panoramic view of the surrounding hills is a 6-inch-tall idol of Hanuman. The main temple has an interior cave adorned with the numerous statues of Lord Hanuman along with his mother, Maa Anjani. Ram Navami and Hanuman Jayanti, which celebrate the birth of Lord Ram and Lord Hanuman respectively.

WEATHER : 27 - 37°C

Tags : Temple

Timings : 8:00 AM to 11:00 AM

4:30 PM to 9:00 PM

Aarti Timings

Summers - 8:00 AM to 9:00 AM and 7:00 PM to 8:00 PM

Winters - 8:30 AM to 9:30 AM and 6:30 PM to 7:30 PM

Kanak Bhawan, Ayodhya Overview

The Kanak Bhawan is established towards the northeastern corner of the Ram Janmabhoomi in Tulsi Nagar. Constructed in 1891, this temple is also known as Sone-ka-Ghar. It is a holy site dedicated to the Hindu deity Lord Rama and his wife, Goddess Sita.

Kanak Bhawan, also meaning Golden Palace, cites three golden-crowned idols of the two gods under a silver roof in the sanctum santorum (Garbagriha). It is believed that this shrine was gifted to Rama and Sita by the former's stepmother, Kaikeyi.

Upon designed renovation during Vikramaditya's reign, the present site was further entirely revamped by Vrish Bhanu Kunwari. This Bundela-styled temple is currently managed by the Sri Vrishbhan Dharma Setu Trust Private Limited

Weather : 27 - 37°C

Tags : Temple

Timings : 5:00 AM to 8:00 PM

Aarti Timings

5:00 AM to 6:00 AM and 8:00 PM to 8:30 PM

Nageshwarnath Temple, Ayodhya Overview

Established in the name of the local deity, Lord Nageshwarnath, the Nageshwarnath Temple is located adjacent to the Theri Bazaar in Ayodhya. It is believed to have been set up by Kush or Kusha, Lord Rama's son.

Although this sacred site continued to be in good maintenance since 750 AD, the current temple is said to have been reconstructed in 1750 by Safar Jung's minister, Naval Rai. Legend has it that Kush came across a Shiva devotee called Naga Kanya when he happened to lose his arm ring in the local bath.

Upon learning that the latter had fallen in love with him, he raised this Shaiva temple for Naga Kanya. The Nageshwarnath Temple attracts numerous devotees during Mahashivaratri and Trayodashi, also known as Pradosh Vrat or Pradosh Vratam, in Southern India. The Shiva Barat or the procession of Lord Shiva is a significant attraction here.

Weather : 27 - 37°C

Tags : Garden & Park

Timings : 4:00 AM to 7:00 PM

Entry Fee : None

Gulab Bari, Ayodhya Overview

Also known as the Garden of Roses, the Gulab Bari is situated in Vaidehi Nagar. It is the tomb of the third Nawab of Faizabad (Oudh or Awadh), Nawab Shuja-ud-Daula and his parents.

The 18th-century structure of the Gulab Bari brings out pure Nawab-styled architecture alongside a vast array of rose species in addition to fountains and lush greenery. Listed under the Ancient Monuments and Archaeological Sites and Remains Act, Gulab Bari is currently preserved as a part of national heritage.

Weather : 27 - 37°C

Tags : Temple

Timings : Treta Ke Thakur is open for 24 hours on the day of the Ekadashi. It usually takes place during November.

Treta Ke Thakur, Ayodhya Overview

Situated along the Naya Ghat of Ayodhya, the Treta Ke Thakur Temple houses numerous idols including that of Lord Ram, Sita, Lakshman, Hanuman, Bharat and Sugreev. These statues are said to have been sculpted out of a single black sandstone.

Treta Ke Thakur is believed to have been constructed 300 years into the past, by Kullu, the king of the time. It is said that this structure stands on the very same ground of the famous Ashwamedha Yagna performed by Lord Rama. The temple was further revamped in the 1700s by the Maratha queen of the time, Ahilyabai Holkar.

It is open to the public only once a year on a day marked as the Ekadashi. This day is observed on the Shukla Paksha's eleventh day during the month of Karthika according to the Hindu calendar. Colourful celebrations alongside preserved traditional customs are carried out on this day.

The Lata Mangeshkar Chowk[1] in the heart of Ayodhya has become a stop for many locals and tourists who use the roundabout to go to the site of the under-construction Ram

Temple. Constructed by the Uttar Pradesh government to honour the legendary singer on her 93rd birth anniversary, the chowk was inaugurated by Prime Minister Narendra Modi virtually on September 28. "The roundabout reflects the grandeur of what Ayodhya is going to be developed into along with the Ram temple. It is also such a great tribute to Lata Mangeshkar ji. We all are truly delighted to see it," Mahendra Rana, a tourist from Una in Madhya Pradesh, said.

LOCATED ON THE ROAD leading to Faizabad, the chowk connects the Saryu Ghat (Naya Ghat) on one side and the Ram Path, which leads to the site of the under-construction Ram temple, on the other. It is here that most visitors start their tour

---

1.   https://www.hindustantimes.com/cities/lucknow-news/upcminaugurates-lata-mangeshkar-chowk-in-ayodhya-in-honour-of-legendary-singer-101664353991443.html

of the city and their journey to the temple. Ram bhajans by Lata Mangeshkar play on speakers in a loop as tourists evade traffic to walk up to the chowk. Some stand on the outside boundary while others cross over inside to take pictures and selfies before leaving for their onward journey.

Jhansi resident Abhishek Pal Singh along with his family members made a brief halt at the roundabout. "We have come to Ayodhya after four years. The chowk is a welcome change. The last time this place was choked with traffic. After taking some pictures here, we will visit the Ram temple and attend the aarti at the Saryu ghat in the evening," he said. The Lata Mangeshkar Chowk, constructed with red sandstone, skirts a small tank at the centre of which rises the huge veena, inviting curiosity from onlookers. The instrument holds an important place in Indian classical music and is known as the instrument of Goddess Saraswati. Inside the small tank are 92 white marble lotuses symbolising the 92-year-long life of Lata Mangeshkar.

Ram Mandir, Ayodhya Overview

"The birthplace of Lord Rama"

Ayodhya Tourism

Often referred to as the birthplace of Lord Rama, Ayodhya is deeply entrenched in Hindu mythology and spirituality. Nestled along the banks of the sacred Sarayu River in Uttar Pradesh, Ayodhya stands first among the seven most sacred pilgrimage sites for Hindus. The name "Ayodhya" itself is deeply intertwined with the Ramayana in which it was known as the capital of the ancient Kosala Kingdom. The Ramayana immortalized Ayodhya through its association with the epic tale of Lord Rama. This ancient city holds immense significance for millions of Hindus, serving as a pilgrimage site where devotees pay homage to Lord Rama and seek spiritual solace.

AT THE HEART OF AYODHYA lies the newly inaugurated Ram Temple[2], a monumental structure that stands as a symbol of devotion and faith. Many Hindus believe that it is located at the site of Ram Janmabhoomi, the mythical birthplace of Rama, a principal deity of Hinduism. On 22 January 2024, amidst great pomp and celebration, the Ram Temple was inaugurated, marking a historic moment for Hindu devotees around the world. Upon completion, the temple complex became the world's third-largest Hindu temple. Balak Ram or the Infant form of Rama is the presiding deity of the temple which is an

2. https://www.holidify.com/places/ayodhya/ramjanma-bhoomi-sightseeing-1253.html

architectural marvel drawing pilgrims seeking blessings in his divine presence.

One of the most anticipated events in Ayodhya is the Ayodhya Deepotsav, a grand festival celebrated with great fervor and enthusiasm. Started in 2017, the festival is celebrated around Diwali. During this festival, the entire city is illuminated with millions of earthen lamps, breaking the Guinness World Record with over 22.23 lakh diyas lit up on Ram ki Paidi. Additionally, Ayodhya is esteemed in Jainism, as it marks the birthplace of four of the religion's 24 Tirthankaras[3]. Pilgrims and tourists flock to this ancient city to pay homage to Lord Rama and explore the myriad temples, shrines, ghats, and historical sites that dot its landscape.

TRANSLATING TO RAM'S Birthplace, the Ram Janmabhoomi is believed to have been the birthplace of the Hindu deity, Lord Ram. According to the Indian epic Ramayan, Ram, Lord Vishnu's seventh manifestation, is said to have grown

---

3.   https://www.holidify.com/collections/jain-temples-in-india

up along Ayodhya's river Sarayu. Located in the ancient city of Ayodhya, he Ram Janmabhoomi is a highly revered site for Hindu devotees.

The significance of Ram Janmabhoomi Ayodhya stems primarily from its association with the epic Hindu scripture, the Ramayana. According to this ancient text, Ayodhya was the capital of the kingdom of Kosala and the birthplace of Lord Rama, who was born to King Dasharatha and Queen Kaushalya. The story of Rama's life, his exile, and eventual return to Ayodhya forms the essence of the Ramayana, making Ayodhya a focal point of pilgrimage and devotion for Hindus.

After being a conflicted site for decades, the Ram Janmabhoomi land was handed over to a trust by the Supreme Court of India to build the Ram Temple. The groundbreaking ceremony for laying of the foundation stone for the Ram Temple of Ayodhya was performed on 5 August 2020 by Prime Minister Narendra Modi. The proposed design of the temple is grand and magnificent.

The construction of the Ram Temple at Ram Janmabhoomi Ayodhya commenced in 2020 and was completed in January 22, 2024. The temple complex is envisioned to be a grand architectural marvel, designed to accommodate millions of pilgrims and devotees from around the world. It is expected to serve as a symbol of unity, spirituality, and cultural heritage for generations to come.

Today, Ram Janmabhoomi Ayodhya continues to be a site of immense religious significance and pilgrimage for Hindus worldwide. It stands as a testament to the enduring legacy of Lord Rama and the rich cultural heritage of India.

Must Know Before You Visit Ram Mandir

Note :

- Devotees can enter the Shri Ram Janmabhoomi Mandir for Darshan from 6:30 am to 9:30 pm.

- The entire process from entry to exit after Darshan at the Shri Ram Janmabhoomi Mandir is simple and convenient, typically taking 60 to 75 minutes.

- To streamline their visit, devotees are advised to leave their mobile phones, footwear, purses, etc., outside the Mandir premises.

- Devotees are requested not to bring flowers, garlands, prasad, etc., to the Shri Ram Janmabhoomi Mandir.

- Entry for Mangala Aarti at 4 am, Shringar Aarti at 6:15 am, and Shayan Aarti at 10 pm requires an entry pass, which can be obtained for free from the website of the Shri Ram Janmabhoomi Teerth Kshetra Trust.

- Information such as the devotee's name, age, Aadhar card, mobile number, and city is required for the entry pass.

- There is no arrangement for a special darshan by paying a certain fee or through any special pass at the Shri Ram Janmabhoomi Mandir. Any such claims are likely scams.

- Wheelchairs are available within the Mandir premises for the elderly and differently-abled. These wheelchairs are free of charge, but a nominal fee is payable to the young volunteer assisting with the wheelchair.

After getting darshan in Hannuan and Ayodya Temple, you can really have good meal in the South Indian Café and take rest.

Day 3 : Ayodya Tour Extended

Day-3 will start with having a good morning meal at Soth Indian café and proceeding to your tour.

Ayodhya Deepotsav, Ayodhya Overview

Ayodhya Deepotsav is an annual festival celebrated in the holy city of Ayodhya, Uttar Pradesh, India. The festival holds great cultural and religious significance as it commemorates the return of Lord Rama to Ayodhya after his 14-year exile and his victory over the demon king Ravana. Deepotsav, which translates to "festival of lights," is celebrated with grandeur and enthusiasm, drawing devotees and tourists from all over the country.

One of the highlights of Ayodhya Deepotsav is the lighting of millions of earthen lamps (diyas) along the banks of the Saryu River and throughout the city. The entire city is illuminated with the glow of countless lamps, creating a mesmerizing spectacle that symbolizes the victory of light over darkness and good over evil. The lighting of diyas is accompanied by elaborate decorations, cultural performances, and religious ceremonies, adding to the festive atmosphere.

The grandeur and spiritual significance of Ayodhya Deepotsav have made it a symbol of India's cultural and religious heritage, attracting visitors and pilgrims from different parts of the world. The festival exemplifies the spirit of Diwali, the festival of lights, and reinforces the timeless message of righteousness and compassion embodied by Lord Rama. Ayodhya Deepotsav not only celebrates the glory of Lord Rama's return but also serves as a reminder of the enduring values that continue to inspire millions of people worldwide.

Weather : 27 - 37°C

Tags : Temple

Timings : Sunrise - Sunset

Time Required : 1 - 2 hrs

Entry Fee : No Entry Fee

Raja Mandir , Ayodhya Overview

Located on the banks of river Ghaggar (Sarayu) in Guptar Ghar, Raja Mandir in Faizabad has been associated with numerous mythological stories time and again. The temple houses stunningly carved idols of many Hindu Gods and Goddess, which are ornamentally clad in silken fabrics and rich jewellery.

The exquisite construction of the temple reflects the brilliance of Hindu architecture. Once known for its association with Lord Sri Ram, the ruler of Ayodhya; the shrine is now a regular temple with statues of numerous deities.

The location of Raja Mandir just on the brink of the river makes a mesmerising reflection of the shrine in the waters which is a beholding sight for the eyes. The umpteen devotees who throng the place all year round, also believe that a dip in the holy waters of the river can cleanse their souls of all sins.

Weather : 27 - 37°C

Tags : Amusement & Theme Park

Timings : Sunrise - Sunset

Time Required : 1 - 2 hrs

Entry Fee : No Entry Fee

Ramkatha Park, Ayodhya Overview

Ram Katha Park is a beautiful park in Ayodhya, housing open-air theatres and well-kept lawns. Spread over a vast area of land, it is a popular venue for the devotional programmes, cultural performances, religious events, dance, poetry and katha recital sessions.

On evenings, which are free of any occasions, Ram Katha Park is used as a playground for kids or a leisure garden for adults. It also promotes both cultural and pop events and encourages national as well as international artists to showcase their talents. It has become a common favourite as the airy amphitheatre is a respite from the crowded and the congested halls of the city.

Weather : 27 - 37°C

Tags : Temple

Timings : 8:00 AM - 12:00 PM, 4:00 PM - 10:00 PM

Time Required : 1 - 2 hrs

Dashrath Bhavan, Ayodhya Overview

Located in the heart of the city, in Ramkot Ayodhya, in Faizabad; Dashrath Bhavan is the original residence of King Dashrath- the ruler of Ayodhya and father to Lord Sri Ram. Popularly known as Bada Asthan or Badi Jagah, Dashrath Mahal houses magnificent shrines of King Ram.

Believed to have housed Lord Rama's childhood and King Dasharath's capital, this pretty palace hosts a decorated and ornamented entrance with beautiful paintings. Within the palace, there are saffron-clad monks chanting mantras, singing and dancing.

Although relatively smaller than the superlative of a palace, the Dashrath Bhavan is a definite magnet during festivities such as Ram Vivah, Karthik Mela, Diwali, Ram Navami and Shravan Mela.

Weather : 27 - 37°C

Tags : Temple

Timings : Sunrise - Sunset

Time Required : 1 - 2 hrs

Mani Parbat, Ayodhya Overview

Situated about 65 feet above sea level, Mani Parbat is a tiny hillock situated in Kami Ganj, Ayodhya. Besides being a great city viewpoint, the Parbat also houses a stupa built by Emperor Ashoka and a Buddhist monastery.

Housing a line of religious shrines, Mani Parbat is located quite close to another hilly mound called the Sugriv Parbat. There is an Islamic mausoleum at the foothills of Mani Parbat.

Guptar Ghat, Ayodhya Overview

Situated on the banks of river Sarayu, also known as Ghaggar, Guptar Ghat is a revered site in Faizabad near Ayodhya. With a flight of steps leading to the holy river, this ghat was once the neighbour of the colonial Company Gardens, which is now known as the Gupta Ghat Van.

This place is said to be the place where the Hindu deity Lord Ram meditated and undertook the 'Jal Samadhi' in the river. After which, he attained 'Baikuntha' and descended into heaven as an avatar of Lord Vishnu.

Among the several temples situated here, the Sita- Ram temple, Chakrahari shrine and the Narsingh temple are popular. Revamped in the 1800s and constantly improvised by the UP

Government, the Guptar Ghat is currently equipped with modern amenities as well.

Try to complete these places before 4.00 p.m. and then come to Dharamshala, vacate the room and proceed to Ayodhya Dham Railway station.

Board the Train to Varanasi by Vande Bharat Express Train No. 22346 Departure Time 05.20 p.m. AC Chair car including Evening Snack / Dinner.

Again why I choose this train is the convenience that it had offered. After 3 days of roaming in the streets I found an attractive tour to Varanasi with all the facilities included in the train and so I booked by this train. You can book the train that you like the most.

Once I got into the train, It served with all the facilities that a traveller to possess including the announcement of the station that its going to in the coming stations.

Accordingly it had all the facilities that it could have including serving of important snacks and dishes that it could have in just Rs. 878.15 per person in ITCTC Booking. The total journey of the train is only 2 Hours and 40 Minutes and in this travel time, they gave snacks and beverages and also one full fledged meal for those getting down at Varanasi. We were full and had completed our Dinner out there with family.

So the train reached Varanasi and we got down at Varanasi railway station and went to the hotel nearby.

So the Day 3 of the Trip was completed successfully.

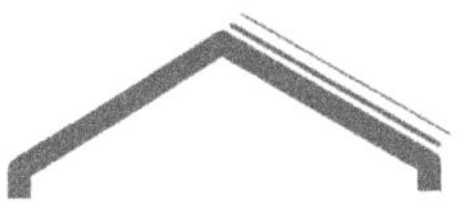

Day : 4 Trip to Varanasi

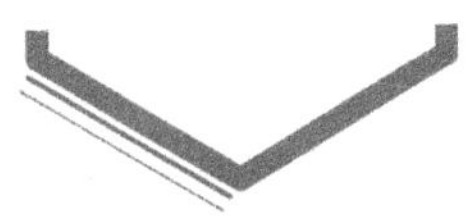

Varanasi, often dubbed as the spiritual capital of India, indeed offers a rich tapestry of experiences for travelers seeking to immerse themselves in its culture and spirituality. Here are some must-visit places in Varanasi:

1. **Banaras Ghats:** The ghats of Varanasi are the heart and soul of the city. Witness the devout performing rituals and ceremonies along the banks of the Ganges River. The Dashashwamedh Ghat is particularly famous for its evening Ganga Aarti, a mesmerizing ritual involving fire and chanting.

2. **Manikarnika Ghat**: This ghat is one of the most sacred and also the principal cremation ground in Varanasi. Witnessing the funeral pyres burning continuously is a poignant and humbling experience, reminding visitors of the cycle of life and death in Hinduism.

3. **Banaras Hindu University (BHU)** Museum: Explore the rich cultural heritage of India through a vast collection of artifacts, including miniature paintings, sculptures, and archaeological finds. The museum offers insights into the history and artistic traditions of Varanasi and its surrounding regions.

4. **Ruchika Art Gallery:** Engage in a hands-on artistic experience by participating in workshops conducted at Ruchika Art Gallery. Learn traditional art forms such as Madhubani

painting or try your hand at pottery under the guidance of skilled artisans.

5. **Vishnu Tea Emporium**: Indulge in a sensory delight at Vishnu Tea Emporium, known for serving some of the finest chai in India. Sample different varieties of tea and purchase souvenirs to savor the flavors of Varanasi long after your visit.

6. **Sarnath**: Just a short drive from Varanasi, Sarnath is a significant Buddhist pilgrimage site where Lord Buddha preached his first sermon after attaining enlightenment. Explore the ancient ruins, visit the Dhamek Stupa, and soak in the tranquil ambiance of this sacred place.

7. **Kashi Vishwanath Temple**: Pay homage to Lord Shiva at one of the holiest Hindu temples in India. The Kashi Vishwanath Temple, dedicated to the Lord of the Universe, attracts millions of devotees each year. Experience the spirituality and devotion that permeate the atmosphere of this revered site.

8. **Bharat Mata Mandir**: Marvel at the unique temple dedicated to Mother India, showcasing a relief map of the Indian subcontinent carved in marble. The temple symbolizes the unity and diversity of India and is a tribute to the nation's cultural and geographical heritage.

These are just a few highlights of what Varanasi has to offer. The city's vibrant streets, bustling markets, and myriad temples and shrines provide endless opportunities for exploration and discovery.

THE GANGES RIVER, OFTEN referred to as "Mother Ganga," holds immense cultural and spiritual significance in India. Here's a closer look at its importance and some experiences you can enjoy along its banks in Varanasi:

1. Spiritual Significance: Hindus believe that bathing in the waters of the Ganges cleanses one of sins and facilitates spiritual purification. Varanasi, being one of the oldest and holiest cities in India, attracts pilgrims from all over the world who come to perform rituals, offer prayers, and immerse themselves in the sacred waters of the Ganges.

2. Sunrise Cruise: Witnessing the sunrise over the Ganges is a mesmerizing experience. Negotiate with a boatman at one of

the ghats to take you on a serene cruise along the river as the golden hues of dawn illuminate the ancient city. The tranquility of the river at dawn is truly captivating and offers a unique perspective of Varanasi waking up to a new day.

3. Floating Offerings: Purchase a small floating offering adorned with fresh flowers and a candle from vendors along the ghats. As you release it onto the Ganges, watch it drift along the river, symbolizing your reverence and connection to Hindu culture. The serene act of releasing these offerings is a deeply spiritual and memorable experience that allows you to connect with the traditions and rituals of Varanasi.

4.Ghat Activities: Spend time exploring the various ghats lining the riverbank. From observing devout Hindus performing rituals to witnessing the vibrant life unfolding along the ghats, there's much to see and experience. Engage with locals, observe the daily activities, and soak in the atmosphere of devotion and spirituality that permeates the riverfront.

5. Boat Ride at Sunset: In the late afternoon or early evening, consider taking another boat ride, this time to witness the mesmerizing Ganga Aarti ceremony at one of the ghats, such as Dashashwamedh Ghat. As dusk descends, the ghats come alive

with the sound of prayers, music, and chants, creating a magical ambiance that reflects the spiritual essence of Varanasi.

6. Ganga Arti Experience: Attend the Ganga Aarti ceremony, a spectacular ritual where priests offer prayers to the river with fire and incense, accompanied by chanting and music. The rhythmic movements of the priests, the flickering flames, and the collective devotion of the gathered crowd create a captivating spectacle that leaves a lasting impression.

Exploring Varanasi along the banks of the Ganges offers a profound and enriching experience that immerses you in the spiritual and cultural heritage of India.

The **Dasaswamedh** Ghat is indeed a vibrant and bustling hub of activity in Varanasi, offering visitors a captivating glimpse into the city's rich culture and spiritual traditions. Here's what you can expect when you visit this iconic ghat:

1. Lively Atmosphere: From flower vendors to boat operators and colorful sadhus, Dasaswamedh Ghat is teeming with energy and activity throughout the day. Immerse yourself in the lively atmosphere as you explore the bustling marketplace and observe the diverse array of people and vendors along the riverbank.

2.Ganga Aarti Ceremony: One of the highlights of visiting Dasaswamedh Ghat is witnessing the enchanting Ganga Aarti ceremony that takes place every evening. As dusk descends, the ghat comes alive with the sounds of chanting, music, and the aroma of incense. Hindu priests clad in saffron robes perform intricate rituals, offering prayers and blessings to the sacred river. The sight of the illuminated lamps and the rhythmic movements of the priests create a mesmerizing spectacle that leaves a profound impression on visitors.

3. Crowd Tips: To ensure a prime viewing spot for the Ganga Aarti ceremony, it's advisable to arrive at the ghat well in advance, especially during peak tourist seasons. By arriving a couple of hours early, you can secure a favorable position and avoid the crowds. Alternatively, consider watching the ceremony from a boat on the Ganges or from the balconies of nearby shops, which offer unique vantage points for capturing the spectacle.

4. Boat Ride: For a different perspective of the Ganga Aarti ceremony, consider taking a boat ride along the Ganges. From the water, you can witness the illuminated ghats and the mesmerizing rituals unfolding against the backdrop of the evening sky. Boat operators can provide insight into the significance of the ceremony and ensure a memorable experience on the river.

5. Cultural Immersion: Beyond the spectacle of the Ganga Aarti, Dasaswamedh Ghat offers an opportunity to immerse yourself in the rich tapestry of Varanasi's culture and traditions. Engage with locals, explore the nearby temples and markets, and soak in the spiritual ambiance of this historic ghat.

Visiting Dasaswamedh Ghat is an essential part of experiencing the essence of Varanasi, where spirituality, tradition, and vibrant street life converge along the sacred banks of the Ganges.

Assi Ghat indeed offers a unique blend of spirituality, cultural activities, and serene ambiance, making it a must-visit destination in Varanasi. Here's a closer look at what makes Assi Ghat a standout attraction:

1. Sacred Lingam and Fig Tree: At the heart of Assi Ghat lies a revered Shiva lingam nestled beneath a sacred fig tree. This ancient symbol of Lord Shiva attracts scores of devotees who come to offer prayers and seek blessings after bathing in the holy waters of the Ganges. The tranquil surroundings of Assi Ghat provide the perfect setting for spiritual contemplation and worship.

2. Morning Yoga Sessions: Start your day on a rejuvenating note by participating in free morning yoga classes held at Assi Ghat. Join fellow enthusiasts in practicing yoga postures, led by experienced instructors, against the backdrop of the serene river. The soothing sounds of live music enhance the meditative experience, allowing you to harmonize your mind, body, and spirit amidst the tranquil ambiance of Assi Ghat.

3. Evening Ganga Aarti: Experience the enchanting Ganga Aarti ceremony at Assi Ghat in the evening, a slightly smaller and more intimate affair compared to the one at Dasaswamedh Ghat. As dusk descends, witness the mesmerizing rituals performed by priests, accompanied by devotional songs and the flickering flames of oil lamps. The serene atmosphere of Assi Ghat provides a serene setting for connecting with the spiritual essence of Varanasi.

4. Cultural Exchange: Assi Ghat serves as a melting pot of cultures, attracting travelers from around the world who come

to immerse themselves in the vibrant tapestry of Varanasi's traditions and customs. Engage in conversations with fellow visitors and locals, explore nearby cafes and markets, and soak in the cultural diversity that defines the spirit of Assi Ghat.

5. Riverfront Promenade: Take a leisurely stroll along the riverfront promenade of Assi Ghat, offering panoramic views of the Ganges and the city skyline. Witness the daily activities unfolding along the ghats, from ritual baths to colorful ceremonies, and capture the essence of life along the sacred river.

Visiting Assi Ghat offers a transformative journey of self-discovery, spirituality, and cultural immersion, making it a memorable highlight of any trip to Varanasi.

Manikarnika Ghat stands as a profound testament to the cycle of life and death in Hinduism, offering visitors a glimpse into the sacred rituals surrounding cremation and the pursuit of spiritual liberation. Here's a deeper insight into the significance of Manikarnika Ghat and how to approach this solemn yet culturally rich experience:

1. Spiritual Significance: Hindus believe that cremation at Manikarnika Ghat holds immense spiritual significance, as it is believed to facilitate the soul's journey towards moksha, or liberation from the cycle of reincarnation. The perpetually burning funeral pyres symbolize the eternal nature of life and death, serving as a poignant reminder of the impermanence of existence.

2. Guided Tours: While exploring Manikarnika Ghat, you may encounter priests or guides offering to lead you through the site and provide insights into the rituals and traditions associated with cremation. However, it's essential to exercise caution, as some individuals may be overly aggressive in soliciting money

from tourists. Be discerning in your interactions and opt for guides who respect your boundaries and offer genuine cultural insights.

3. Observing Cremations: Visitors may have the opportunity to witness cremations up close, either by paying a fee or through guided tours. While this experience can be deeply profound, it's essential to approach it with sensitivity and respect. Be mindful of the solemnity of the occasion and refrain from taking photographs out of respect for the deceased and their grieving families.

4. Boat Tours: If witnessing cremations up close feels overwhelming, consider viewing Manikarnika Ghat from a distance during a boat tour along the Ganges River. This allows you to observe the rituals from a more detached perspective while still gaining an understanding of the cultural and spiritual significance of the site.

5. Cultural Sensitivity: When visiting Manikarnika Ghat or any other sacred site in Varanasi, it's crucial to adhere to cultural norms and practices. Dress modestly, maintain a respectful demeanor, and refrain from engaging in disruptive behavior. Remember that you are participating in a deeply sacred and solemn ritual, and your conduct should reflect reverence and understanding.

Manikarnika Ghat offers a profound and humbling insight into the spiritual beliefs and practices of Hinduism, serving as a poignant reminder of the interconnectedness of life and death. Approach this experience with an open heart and mind, honoring the sanctity of the rituals and the profound significance they hold for millions of people.

Sarnath, located just a short distance from Varanasi, holds immense significance in the history of Buddhism and offers visitors a fascinating glimpse into the life and teachings of Lord Buddha. Here's what you can explore during a day trip to Sarnath:

1. Dhamek Stupa: Standing tall and majestic, the Dhamek Stupa is a testament to the rich Buddhist heritage of Sarnath. Believed to be the site where Lord Buddha delivered his first sermon after attaining enlightenment, the stupa is adorned with intricate carvings depicting various motifs such as birds, people, and flowers. Take a leisurely stroll around the stupa and soak in the spiritual ambiance of this ancient monument.

2. Chaukhandi Stupa: Explore the Chaukhandi Stupa, an ancient Buddhist shrine dating back to at least the 6th century. This octagonal structure serves as a reminder of Sarnath's significance as a pilgrimage site for Buddhists worldwide. Marvel at the architectural intricacies of the stupa and contemplate its historical and cultural significance.

3. Sarnath Museum: Delve into the rich history and heritage of Sarnath at the Sarnath Museum, home to a diverse collection of artifacts and sculptures dating back to the ancient Mauryan and Gupta periods. Admire the famous Lion Capital of Ashoka, a masterpiece of ancient Indian art that once adorned the Ashoka Pillar and now serves as the National Emblem of India.

4. Tibetan Temple: Experience the serenity of the Tibetan Temple, nestled amidst the bustling market of Sarnath. Pay homage to Lord Buddha and immerse yourself in the peaceful ambiance of this sacred site, which serves as a spiritual haven for Tibetan Buddhists and visitors seeking solace and reflection.

5. Exploration and Contemplation: Take the time to explore the tranquil surroundings of Sarnath, wandering through its lush gardens and ancient ruins. Reflect on the profound teachings of Lord Buddha as you contemplate the significance of this sacred pilgrimage site.

A day trip to Sarnath from Varanasi offers a transformative journey into the heart of Buddhism, allowing you to connect with the spiritual legacy of Lord Buddha and experience the timeless beauty of this historic pilgrimage destination.

The Shri Kashi Vishwanath Temple, also known as the Golden Temple, stands as a symbol of devotion and architectural splendor in Varanasi. Here's what you can expect when visiting this revered Hindu pilgrimage site:

1. Architectural Marvel: The Shri Kashi Vishwanath Temple is renowned for its magnificent architecture, particularly its striking spire plated with around 800 kilograms of pure gold. The temple's distinctive design has inspired countless other temples across India, making it a cultural icon revered by devotees and tourists alike.

2. Security Measures: Due to the temple's significance and high footfall of visitors, strict security measures are in place to ensure the safety and sanctity of the complex. Tourists are required to store their belongings, including cameras, phones, and bags, in rentable lockers nearby. Foreign visitors may need to verify their passports and visas at the Darshan Booking Desk before entering the temple premises.

3. Devotional Experience: Prepare for a spiritually enriching experience as you join the queue of devotees waiting to enter the sanctum sanctorum of the temple. Upon reaching the inner sanctum, you'll have the opportunity to offer prayers and seek

blessings from the sacred Shiva lingam, believed to absolve sins and grant divine grace to devotees. The atmosphere inside the temple is charged with devotion and reverence, offering a profound and unforgettable experience for visitors.

4. Crowd Management: To avoid long waits and overcrowding, it's advisable to plan your visit to the Shri Kashi Vishwanath Temple during non-peak hours and avoid Hindu holidays when devotee turnout is exceptionally high. Arriving early in the morning or later in the evening may offer a more peaceful and conducive atmosphere for prayer and contemplation. We planned out trip to Kasi Vishwanath Temple only during 04.00 am in the morning so that there is no requirement of crowd.

5. Cultural Insights: Take the time to appreciate the intricate artwork and architectural details adorning the temple complex, reflecting the rich cultural heritage of Varanasi and Hinduism. Engage with local priests and devotees to gain deeper insights into the significance of the temple and its rituals, fostering a greater understanding and appreciation of Indian spirituality.

Visiting the Shri Kashi Vishwanath Temple is a transformative journey that allows you to connect with the divine and experience the profound spirituality that permeates the sacred city of Varanasi. Approach this revered pilgrimage site with humility, respect, and an open heart, and you're sure to be rewarded with a memorable and spiritually uplifting experience.

Banaras Hindu University (BHU) stands as a beacon of academic excellence and cultural heritage in Varanasi, offering visitors a tranquil respite from the bustling city streets. Here's what you can explore during a visit to this prestigious institution:

1. Lush Campus: Spread across 1,300 acres, the BHU campus is a verdant oasis adorned with tall trees and green spaces, providing a serene retreat from the hustle and bustle of Varanasi. Take a leisurely stroll through the campus grounds, soaking in the natural beauty and peaceful ambiance that surrounds you.

2. New Vishwanath Temple: Marvel at the architectural grandeur of the New Vishwanath Temple, a towering structure that stands as a testament to the rich cultural heritage of Varanasi. Drawing inspiration from the iconic Shri Kashi Vishwanath Temple, this magnificent temple offers visitors a glimpse into the spiritual legacy of the region.

3. Bharat Kala Bhavan Museum: Delve into the rich artistic and archaeological heritage of India at the Bharat Kala Bhavan Museum, housed within the BHU campus. Explore a vast collection of miniature paintings, sculptures, textiles, and artifacts spanning centuries of Indian history and culture. From ancient relics to contemporary masterpieces, the museum offers a comprehensive insight into the artistic traditions of India.

4. Cultural Immersion: Immerse yourself in the vibrant cultural milieu of BHU, where students from diverse backgrounds come together to pursue academic excellence and creative pursuits. Engage with faculty members and students to gain insights into the university's academic programs, research initiatives, and cultural activities, fostering a deeper understanding of its significance in the educational landscape of India.

5. Academic Excellence: BHU is renowned for its academic programs across various disciplines, including arts, sciences, engineering, and medicine. Take the opportunity to attend

lectures, seminars, or cultural events hosted by the university, gaining valuable knowledge and insights from esteemed faculty members and scholars.

A visit to Banaras Hindu University offers a multifaceted experience encompassing natural beauty, architectural splendor, cultural enrichment, and academic excellence. Whether you're a student, scholar, or visitor, the university's serene campus and rich heritage are sure to leave a lasting impression on your mind and soul.

The Shri Durga Temple, affectionately known as the "Monkey Temple," offers a unique spiritual experience just a stone's throw away from Assi Ghat in Varanasi. Here's what you can expect when visiting this vibrant and sacred site:

1. Dedication to Goddess Durga: The Shri Durga Temple is dedicated to the Hindu goddess Durga, revered as the embodiment of divine feminine power and protection. Hindus visit this temple to pay homage to Goddess Durga and seek her blessings for courage, strength, and protection from adversity.

2. Vibrant Red Architecture: The temple's striking red façade, painted from top to bottom, makes it an unmistakable landmark in Varanasi. The vibrant color symbolizes auspiciousness and devotion, inviting visitors to enter and immerse themselves in the spiritual ambiance of the temple.

3. Monkey Encounters: True to its nickname, the "Monkey Temple" is home to a playful troupe of monkeys that roam the temple premises. Visitors may encounter these mischievous creatures as they swing from trees and rooftops, adding a touch of lively charm to the spiritual atmosphere of the temple.

4. Swan Sanctuary: Amidst the hustle and bustle of Varanasi, the Shri Durga Temple provides a serene oasis with a tranquil

pool of water outside its premises. Here, visitors may spot graceful swans gliding across the water, offering a moment of tranquility and serenity amidst the vibrant surroundings.

5. Spiritual Retreat: Whether you're seeking solace, blessings, or simply a moment of quiet contemplation, the Shri Durga Temple provides a sanctuary for spiritual seekers and devotees alike. Take the time to offer prayers, participate in rituals, or simply soak in the divine energy of the temple surroundings.

Visiting the Shri Durga Temple offers a unique opportunity to connect with the divine feminine energy of Goddess Durga and experience the vibrant spirituality that permeates the sacred city of Varanasi. With its vivid red architecture, playful monkeys, and serene swan sanctuary, this temple is a testament to the rich cultural tapestry of the region and the enduring devotion of its devotees.

Ramnagar Fort, located about 14 kilometers from the city center of Varanasi, offers visitors a fascinating blend of history, culture, and quirky charm. Here's what you can explore when visiting this historic landmark:

1. 18th-Century Sandstone Fort: Built in the 18th century, Ramnagar Fort stands as a testament to the architectural grandeur of its time. While it may no longer serve its original defensive purpose, the fort's sandstone walls and majestic gates provide a glimpse into its storied past.

2. Quirky Museum: Step into the fort's museum and prepare to be amazed by its eclectic collection of artifacts. From vintage automobiles and elaborate hookahs to antique weapons and jeweled sedan chairs, the museum offers a treasure trove of curiosities that reflect the opulent lifestyle of its former

inhabitants. Don't miss the one-of-a-kind astronomical clock, a fascinating relic that has stood the test of time for over 150 years.

3. Temple Complex: Explore the temples nestled within the precincts of Ramnagar Fort, each offering a unique glimpse into the religious heritage of the region. One notable temple honors Veda Vyasa, the revered sage and author of the Mahabharata and other important Hindu epics. Pay your respects at these sacred shrines and immerse yourself in the spiritual ambiance of the fort complex.

4. Cultural Heritage: Ramnagar Fort provides a window into the rich cultural heritage of Varanasi and the surrounding region. Learn about the legacy of the erstwhile Maharajas of Kashi as you wander through the fort's halls and courtyards, gaining insights into their lavish lifestyle and patronage of the arts.

5. Scenic Surroundings: Situated on the banks of the Ganges River, Ramnagar Fort offers panoramic views of the picturesque landscape that surrounds it. Take a leisurely stroll along the fort's ramparts, soaking in the tranquil beauty of the river and the lush greenery that stretches beyond.

Visiting Ramnagar Fort is a journey back in time, allowing you to immerse yourself in the rich history and cultural heritage of Varanasi. Whether you're a history buff, a cultural enthusiast, or simply a curious traveler, the fort's intriguing museum and serene surroundings are sure to leave a lasting impression.

Darbhanga Ghat, with its picturesque setting and stunning backdrop provided by the BrijRama Palace, indeed offers photographers a fantastic opportunity to capture the essence of Varanasi in their shots. Here's why it's a must-visit spot for photographers:

1. Regal Backdrop: The BrijRama Palace, with its grand architecture featuring Greek pillars and rounded balconies, adds a touch of regal elegance to the scene. The palace's historic charm and luxurious ambiance create a captivating backdrop for your photographs, elevating them to a new level of sophistication.

2. Prime Sunrise Spot: Arriving at Darbhanga Ghat at dawn allows photographers to capture the mesmerizing beauty of the sunrise over the Ganges River. The soft hues of dawn paint the sky in a palette of pastel colors, creating a magical ambiance that lends itself perfectly to stunning photography.

3. Unobstructed Views: The spacious layout of Darbhanga Ghat provides photographers with ample space to set up their equipment and capture unobstructed views of the river and surrounding landscape. Whether you prefer wide-angle shots or close-up details, you'll find plenty of opportunities to frame your shots without interference.

4. Varied Perspectives: From the top of the ghat's stairs to the water's edge, Darbhanga Ghat offers photographers a range of perspectives to explore. Experiment with different angles, compositions, and focal lengths to capture unique and compelling images that showcase the beauty and diversity of Varanasi.

5. Historical Significance: Beyond its aesthetic appeal, Darbhanga Ghat holds historical significance as a cultural and spiritual hub in Varanasi. Photographers can capture not only the natural beauty of the sunrise but also the timeless traditions and rituals unfolding along the ghats, providing a deeper narrative to their images.

For photographers seeking to capture the essence of Varanasi in their work, Darbhanga Ghat stands out as a premier location offering stunning vistas, architectural splendor, and rich cultural heritage. Don't miss the opportunity to capture the magic of dawn against the backdrop of the Ganges River at this iconic Varanasi landmark.

The Sankat Mochan Hanuman Temple, situated on the banks of the Assi River in Varanasi, offers visitors a serene sanctuary for spiritual reflection and cultural immersion. Here's why it's a must-visit destination in the city:

1. Divine Connection: The temple holds significant religious importance for devotees of Hinduism, who flock here to pay homage to Lord Hanuman, the monkey god known for his devotion and courage. According to legend, the temple marks the spot where the revered Hindu saint and poet Goswami Tulsidas had a divine vision of Hanuman, further enhancing its spiritual significance.

2. Offerings and Rituals: Visitors to the Sankat Mochan Hanuman Temple often bring offerings of sweets and flowers to offer to the deity, seeking blessings for protection from adversity and the removal of obstacles in their lives. The temple's serene surroundings provide a tranquil setting for prayer, meditation, and participation in religious rituals.

3. Monkey Encounters: Keep a lookout for the playful and mischievous monkeys that inhabit the temple premises, adding a lively charm to the spiritual ambiance of the site. While these monkeys may be entertaining to observe, it's essential to exercise caution and refrain from feeding or approaching them closely.

4. Cultural Festivities: Plan your visit to the Sankat Mochan Hanuman Temple during April or May to coincide with the annual "Sankat Mochan Sangeet Samaroh," a prestigious festival of classical music and dance recitals. Held over several days, this

cultural extravaganza attracts performers from around the world, offering visitors a unique opportunity to immerse themselves in the rich heritage of Indian classical arts.

5. Spiritual Retreat: Whether you're seeking solace, seeking blessings, or simply exploring the cultural heritage of Varanasi, the Sankat Mochan Hanuman Temple provides a peaceful sanctuary amidst the bustling city streets. Take the time to offer prayers, participate in rituals, and soak in the spiritual energy of this sacred pilgrimage site.

Located in the heart of Varanasi, the Sankat Mochan Hanuman Temple beckons visitors with its divine aura, cultural richness, and vibrant atmosphere. Pay a visit to this revered spiritual landmark and experience the timeless allure of Hindu spirituality in the sacred city of Varanasi.

The Vishnu Tea Emporium, nestled just a short walk from Dasaswamedh Ghat in Varanasi, offers tea enthusiasts a delightful opportunity to immerse themselves in the rich culture of Indian chai. Here's why a visit to this charming shop is a must for tea lovers:

1. Culinary Experience: Step into the Vishnu Tea Emporium and embark on a culinary journey into the heart of Indian tea culture. Witness up-close demonstrations of how masala chai, the quintessential Indian beverage, is expertly crafted using a blend of aromatic spices and fresh ingredients. Engage with knowledgeable staff who are passionate about sharing the art of tea-making with visitors.

2. Educational Insights: Gain valuable insights into the intricate process of brewing masala chai as you observe the skilled artisans at work. Learn about the different spices and ingredients used to create the perfect blend of flavors, and discover the cultural significance of chai in Indian society. From the brewing technique to the art of flavor balancing, the Vishnu Tea Emporium offers a hands-on learning experience for tea enthusiasts of all levels.

3. Curated Selection: Browse through the emporium's curated selection of tea and spice blends, carefully sourced from across India. From traditional masala chai to exotic herbal infusions, there's something to suit every palate and preference. Take the opportunity to sample different varieties of tea and spices, guided by the expertise of the shop's staff, before selecting the perfect blend to bring home as a cherished souvenir.

4. No Pressure Environment: Enjoy a relaxed shopping experience at the Vishnu Tea Emporium, where there's no pressure to make a purchase. Take your time exploring the shop's offerings, savoring the aromas and flavors of freshly brewed chai, and engaging in meaningful conversations with fellow tea enthusiasts. Whether you're a seasoned connoisseur or a curious

beginner, the emporium welcomes all visitors with warmth and hospitality.

5. Memorable Souvenir: Treat yourself to a unique and memorable souvenir from your visit to Varanasi by purchasing a selection of tea and spices from the Vishnu Tea Emporium. Each sip of masala chai brewed with these authentic ingredients will transport you back to the bustling streets of Varanasi, evoking fond memories of your culinary adventure in the heart of India.

A visit to the Vishnu Tea Emporium promises an enriching and flavorful experience, where you can deepen your appreciation for the art of chai-making and bring home a taste of India's vibrant tea culture.

Once you are done with the basic outing, multi-outing becomes an additional requirement and other places can be visited as per your needs.

Once you are through with the visit then have dinner in any of the good hotels and leave for the railway station with sound memories, Leave for the train Shiv Ganga Express at 12559 in the 3rd AC with amounting to Rs. 1149/- only. Per head from Banaras to New Delhi. You can catch any train as per your requirement.

Conclusion

As our journey through the sacred cities of Naimisaranyam, Ayodhya, and Varanasi draws to a close, we find ourselves enriched by the tapestry of experiences woven into the fabric of time. From the tranquil forests of Naimisaranyam, where the ancient hymns still resonate, to the legendary streets of Ayodhya, where the echoes of myth and devotion linger, and finally to the timeless ghats of Varanasi, where life and death converge in a dance of eternal renewal — each destination has left an indelible mark on our souls.

In Naimisaranyam, we discovered the serenity of introspection, finding solace amidst the whispering leaves and sacred rituals. Ayodhya, with its grand temples and storied past, awakened within us a sense of reverence and devotion, reminding us of the power of faith to transcend time and space. And in Varanasi, the eternal city of light, we witnessed the cyclical nature of existence, embracing both the joys and sorrows that define the human experience.

As we reflect on our pilgrimage, let us carry with us the wisdom gleaned from these sacred sites — the importance of introspection, the power of devotion, and the acceptance of life's ever-changing rhythms. For in the journey from Naimisaranyam to Ayodhya and finally to Varanasi, we have not only explored the depths of our spirituality but also discovered the timeless beauty of our own souls.

May the memories of our pilgrimage continue to inspire and guide us on our quest for truth and enlightenment, long after we have bid farewell to these sacred cities. And may the blessings of Naimisaranyam, Ayodhya, and Varanasi remain with us always, lighting the path as we journey onward in search of deeper meaning and purpose.

This conclusion ties together the themes and experiences encountered throughout the journey, leaving readers with a sense of fulfillment and reflection.

Thank you for choosing my book! Your support means the world to me. As you embark on this journey through its pages, I sincerely hope it brings you joy, inspiration, and new perspectives.

Your feedback is incredibly valuable to me, so please consider sharing your thoughts and opinions by leaving your email ID for me to reach out. Your reviews help me grow as a writer and ensure that future readers discover the magic within these words. Thank you for being a part of this adventure with me.

| Page

www.ingramcontent.com/pod-product-compliance
Lightning Source LLC
Chambersburg PA
CBHW061400140726
47997CB00003B/1305